**Editorial Project Manager**
Lorin E. Klistoff, M.A.

**Illustrator**
Teacher Created Resources Staff

**Cover Artist**
Brenda DiAntonis

**Managing Editor**
Ina Massler Levin, M.A.

**Creative Director**
Karen J. Goldfluss, M.S. Ed.

**Art Production Manager**
Kevin Barnes

**Art Coordinator**
Renée Christine Yates

**Imaging**
James Edward Grace

*Publisher*

*Mary D. Smith, M.S. Ed.*

# Writing Effective Report Card Comments

- Easy-to-use format • Covers a variety of topics
- Clear, concise, and constructive comments

REPORT CARD

School:

Grade:

Teacher:

Student:

"She demonstrates critical thinking in writing."

"He expresses his ideas clearly."

"She is highly proficient in math."

**Authors**

## Kathy Dickinson Crane and Kathleen Law

## Teacher Created Resources, Inc.
6421 Industry Way
Westminster, CA 92683
www.teachercreated.com

ISBN: 978-1-4206-8856-6

© 2007 Teacher Created Resources, Inc.
Made in U.S.A.

Teacher Created Resources

# Table of Contents

# Introduction

A report card is a keepsake that many students will treasure their entire lives! With this thought in mind, the comments a teacher writes on a report card become vital. Report card comments should not only be clear, concise, and constructive, they must also be positive, personal, and powerful.

Report card comments will have an impact on parents, as well as students, so they must be thoughtfully written. A poorly written comment may upset or confuse parents. Instead of receiving parental support, you may cause a rift between the parents and the school or damage the relationship between parent and child. Rather than saying "John is failing math," you can choose comments from this book to state, "John is a fun-loving and happy boy, but he is struggling in math. He needs to work every night, beginning with the multiplication facts through the fives. Please help him review these facts at home." With the comments in this book, you can always take a positive approach or suggest a possible solution. This will strengthen the connection with your student's parents and help you achieve your goal of improving student performance.

This book is organized in an easy-to-use format. It is divided into specific areas that generally need reporting and benefit from clarification. A teacher should be able to turn to the table of contents to be directed to a specific section to find a ready-made comment. If a comment needs expansion or individualization, the Words and Phrases section should help stimulate thought to write the perfect comment with precision and thoughtfulness.

A teacher's well chosen words will be the exact complement needed to make the report card not only a keepsake, but a useful tool that will stimulate communication between the parent and the child, encourage extra practice, and/or provide parents with concrete, relevant examples of their child's performance and progress in school.

# Assessment Methods

## Why Assess?

From the moment a student enters the classroom, an effective teacher is observing, evaluating, and assessing. A teacher's ultimate desire is for each student to succeed and reach full potential while under his or her care.

Classroom assessments can be formal or informal, but whatever the method, the purpose for any assessment is to inform the teacher so he or she can tailor instruction to the needs of the individual and the group. Armed with this information, a teacher can give every student multiple opportunities for further practice and greater success.

Students are multifaceted! To gain greater insight, teachers should use a wide variety of assessment tools. This provides a broader base from which to collect information related to student success and the curriculum.

To optimize the benefit of assessments, parents can be brought in as partners by using effective reporting systems and communicating comments constructively. This communication should be ongoing, timely, clear, and meaningful.

## Types of Assessments

The following lists different types of assessment:

- <u>Individual Assessments</u>: Both oral and written questions or formal testing methods

- <u>Group Assessments</u>: Focusing on the work of the whole group in a cooperative setting

- <u>Anecdotal Notes or Records</u>: Recording behaviors or specific incidents throughout the day

- <u>Portfolios</u>: A collection of student work showing growth during a specific time period

- <u>Observational Checklist</u>: Keeping track of skills mastered, strengths, and weaknesses

- <u>Teacher/Student Conferences or Workshops</u>: Meeting with students to discuss specific work, writings, etc.

- <u>Projects</u>: Assignments given to develop specific items, written reports, or creations that require independent action

- <u>Inventories</u>: A sampling of skills tested for diagnostic purposes

- <u>Questioning</u>: A variety of questions to evaluate the student's thinking and reasoning skills

# Assessment Methods

## Time To Assess

As a teacher begins to develop approaches for effective student evaluation, consideration must be given to scheduling time to plan, developing assessment instruments, collecting and analyzing data, reporting, and adapting teaching styles to reflect student learning.

Following are a few suggestions to lighten the load of assessment:

- <u>Collaborate with colleagues</u>: Sharing the task lightens the load.

- <u>Share evaluation tasks with students</u>: Create systems of peer tutoring or incorporate self-assessment procedures. Allow students to participate in record keeping.

- <u>Plan effective methods of storing data</u>: Keep organized. Use binders, spreadsheets, or computer programs to keep information in a central location.

- <u>Keep anecdotal records handy</u>: Place the record book in an accessible location. Consider using sticky notes or index cards to help with the management.

- <u>Train students to organize portfolios</u>: Students will benefit from instruction and gain practice in organizing and maintaining a portfolio.

- <u>Record observational checklists in a timely manner</u>: If a behavior or skill is observed, record it!

## Build a Home-School Connection

The reporting of student assessments brings to the parents' attention areas of strengths or weaknesses in a child. Increased dialogue between home and school will create a partnership for student growth and motivation and increase academic success.

# Academic Areas

The school day is filled with a myriad of subject matter. Some students are shining stars in all facets of the school day. Most students, however, tend to excel in some areas more than others. Unfortunately, some students struggle in multiple areas.

Whatever the circumstance of the student, progress needs to be reported. Many will have areas where improvement is needed, and specifics can be given to parents that will allow them to give extra help and support. For others, positive comments may just be the motivator for continued success.

This section is divided into academic categories. Choose an academic subject, and you will find comments tailored to fit your students' needs.

# Handwriting

## Proficient

- _____ has great penmanship and takes pride in his/her work.

- _____ has placed great effort in his/her handwriting. He/she is able to correctly form most of the letters.

- It is a joy to read _____'s handwriting. He/she continues to put forth his/her best effort.

## Making Progress

- _____ has made great effort to better his/her penmanship.

- With extra effort, _____'s handwriting will continue to improve. Please encourage him/her to practice at home.

- It is easy to tell that _____ is ready to improve his/her penmanship. He/she has shown great ability in following directions and seems to give the time necessary for correct letter formation.

## Needs Improvement

- It is challenging to decipher _____'s written work. He/she needs to slow down and try to achieve his/her best handwriting with each assignment.

- _____ seems to find handwriting a challenge. He/she needs considerable practice in letter formation and directionality. I have enclosed a set of handwriting pages; please help _____ complete these at home.

- _____ needs to develop his/her fine motor skills. He/she will benefit from working with small manipulatives to strengthen hand muscles.

# Listening

## Proficient

- _____ is very attentive and listens thoroughly in all settings.

- _____ enjoys listening to stories. It is a joy to read to him/her!

- _____ listens carefully and evaluates what he/she hears.

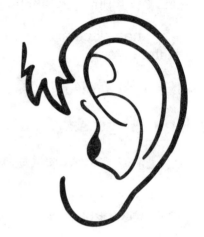

## Making Progress

- _____ has improved in his/her listening. You can continue to increase his/her listening skills by making statements and giving one- or two-step directions that he/she then verbally repeats. This will help _____ focus on the spoken word.

- _____ is becoming a better listener. As a result, he/she is participating more in our discussions.

- _____ has shown increased interest in his/her schoolwork because he/she has improved his/her listening skills.

## Needs Improvement

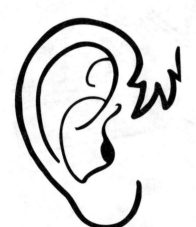

- _____ has a hard time listening. He/she may have an auditory problem; perhaps we should refer him/her for testing.

- _____ has difficulty listening in class and is easily distracted by his/her classmates. He/she needs to listen and concentrate fully on the task at hand.

- _____ does not always listen to instructions because his/her friends easily distract him/her. When he/she listens responsibly, _____ is able to put forth his/her best effort.

# Math

## Proficient

- _____ is highly proficient in math. I am challenging him/her.

- It is apparent that _____ enjoys math. He/she participates in class and can always explain his/her work.

- It is a joy to correct _____'s math work pages. He/she takes pride in his/her work and is very proficient in math.

- _____ can accurately construct and label a variety of graphs.

- _____ can create graphs and explain them to others.

- _____ can apply the knowledge of probability in sports, weather predictions, and games of chance.

- _____ uses appropriate mathematical language. He/she can communicate knowledge clearly and precisely.

- _____ has a positive attitude towards math. He/she can demonstrate the process of addition and subtraction very easily.

- _____ can easily count to _____ .

- _____ is able to demonstrate addition of whole numbers up to 100 with and without regrouping.

- _____ understands and computes story problems with great ease.

- _____ can easily tell time. He/she helps other students willingly with this task.

- _____ can identify all coins and make change with ease.

- _____ understands and applies knowledge of linear measurement. With this knowledge, he/she can accurately apply measurement strategies to successfully solve problems.

- _____ understands place value and can easily regroup multi-digit numbers.

- _____ is successful in comparing and representing numbers using _____ (fractions, decimals, etc.).

- _____ understands and can explain operations in _____.

- _____ can use data analysis and probability to solve problems.

- _____ is successful in comparing, ordering, and representing numbers using _____ (fractions, decimals, factors, or square roots).

- _____ recognizes the relationship among radius, diameter, circumference, and area of a circle. He/she can use related formulas in a problem solving context.

# Math

## Making Progress

- _____ is steadily improving in math. He/she pays attention in class and completes his/her work with few errors. I am pleased with his/her progress.

- _____ has shown increased interest in math. This is reflected in his/her math scores.

- _____ is beginning to interpret graphs, apply that information, and use it in problem solving.

- _____ is gaining confidence when he/she works with graphs. Although he/she needs some assistance, he/she can interpret most graphs with accuracy.

- _____ has memorized all of his/her _____ facts. This impacts his/her ability to complete assignments accurately. Please keep using the flashcards at home each evening to increase speed.

- _____ understands and uses basic math facts up to _____ . Please use the enclosed flashcards to work on the next the level of facts.

- _____ is improving in math, but needs to continue to practice _____ facts.

- Although _____ is doing well in math, he/she is relying too heavily on a (calculator, math chart, etc.) when computing math facts. Please help him/her practice math facts to mastery.

- _____'s work is improving. However, he/she still reverses some numbers.

- _____ can write numbers to 100. Remind him/her to correct reversals when you notice them.

- _____ now knows _____ of the shapes. Continue to practice at home to master this skill.

- _____ can demonstrate addition and subtraction using manipulatives. With practice, he/she will be able to complete problems without concrete support.

- _____ has a better understanding of word problems. He/she participates more in group discussions and is showing more independence in completing assigned story problems.

- Although _____ has made improvement in telling time, he/she needs continued practice.

- _____ is more confident now when manipulating coins. Continue to practice making change at home with him/her.

- With more time and practice, _____ will independently use measurement to solve problems.

- With support, _____ can use manipulatives to represent place value. Further practice will help build independence.

- _____ is more successful at problem solving using a variety of data and probability information.

- _____ is now showing more proficiency in using calculators.

- _____ is now able to explain formulas orally using mathematical vocabulary.

# Math

## Needs Improvement

- _____ is struggling in math. He/she does not seem to enjoy it at all. We need to continue working on basic skills to build a stronger foundation in math.

- _____ is not attentive during math. Perhaps the material is too difficult, and he/she would benefit from additional help at home and at school.

- Encourage _____ to use flashcards and complete all math homework to strengthen skills and develop confidence.

- _____ does not understand the concepts in math. Please call me for an appointment to discuss a plan of action.

- _____ lacks a degree of confidence in math. Extra support and practice at home and at school will build skills and confidence.

- _____ is still struggling with _____ . He/she is relying too heavily on manipulatives and should work on memorizing his/her facts.

- _____ is having difficulty in math. He/she needs to learn the basic facts. Please use the flashcards nightly.

- _____ has/has not memorized all of his/her _____ facts. This impacts _____'s ability to complete assignments accurately.

- I am sorry to report that _____ does not understand the process of _____ . He/she needs additional help. Please call for an appointment.

- _____'s progress in math is not consistent. Although he/she has made some progress, he/she needs to continue reviewing _____ every evening.

- _____ needs considerable adult assistance to complete word problems. He/she cannot explain nor complete his/her work without help. Please continue to provide help and support at home until he/she can work more independently.

- _____ is struggling with telling time. I have sent home a practice clock. Please work with it nightly.

- _____ cannot identify coins. Please practice identifying coins with him/her.

- _____ is unable to successfully demonstrate his/her knowledge when measuring. More practice is needed.

- _____ does not understand place value. Until this is mastered, he/she will have difficulty with the more challenging math problems to come. Please help him/her complete the enclosed place value homework packet.

- _____ is beginning to make progress in _____ . More time and effort is needed, however, to help him/her reach grade level.

- _____ is struggling to make the link between concrete, representational, and abstract.

# Oral Language

## Proficient

- _____ uses complex sentences and expresses his/her ideas clearly.

- _____ has a very high vocabulary, scoring at a _____ grade level. This is apparent in his/her reading, writing, and speaking.

- _____ is a delightful conversationalist; he/she always contributes to our class discussions.

## Making Progress

- _____ speaks with confidence in small groups. With support and practice, this should transfer to a whole-group setting.

- _____ expresses ideas well during conversations, but this is not transferring to our more formal classroom setting. I plan to provide more small and large group opportunities for discussion.

- When _____ answers questions at school, he/she is showing improvement in the use of complete sentences. Please continue to reinforce the use of complete sentences at home.

## Needs Improvement

- _____ has a very limited vocabulary. Please provide opportunities for conversation at home.

- It is difficult to understand _____ . He/she needs to slow down and speak more clearly to be understood.

- _____ is having difficulty when speaking in front of others. We need to find opportunities to encourage practice.

# Reading

## Proficient

- _____ is making excellent progress in reading. He/she is reading well above grade level.

- _____ enjoys reading fiction and nonfiction books. This should benefit him/her in all of the academic areas.

- _____'s love of reading makes him/her a joy to teach.

- _____ is interested in books and reading. He/she often reads for pleasure in class.

- _____ comprehends and follows written directions. He/she is an excellent independent reader.

- _____ learns new vocabulary quickly. This allows him/her to choose and understand more challenging books.

- Because _____ is a great reader, he/she is doing well in all areas.

- _____ asks pertinent questions and participates in story discussions. He/she is a leader in our classroom.

- _____ knows all the letters and sounds of the alphabet. He/she is now beginning to decode words.

- _____ blends short words without assistance. He/she is ready for more challenging words.

- _____ can produce rhymes and identify beginning and ending sounds. He/she is working above grade level in these areas.

- _____ is an independent reader. He/she has a great love for reading that will benefit him/her throughout his/her life.

- _____ is an excellent reader. He/she uses a variety of strategies and self corrects errors.

- _____ is a dynamic, eager reader. His/her insightful comments during class discussions help everyone gain a better understanding of the story.

- _____ has done well this semester. He/she shows great enthusiasm for reading.

- _____ catches on quickly to new reading skills. This is helping him/her become a proficient reader.

- _____ excels in reading. He/she is willing to take risks and choose challenging books to read.

- I am pleased with the progress that _____ has made in reading. His/her strong skills and solid foundation have made him/her a great reader.

- It is a delight to listen to _____ read. He/she reads clearly and with expression.

# Reading

## Proficient *(cont.)*

- _____ enjoys reading poetry and short stories aloud in groups. This is helping other students discover the joy of reading.

- I enjoy reading _____'s summaries. They are very detailed.

- _____ effectively communicates the main idea of a story and summarizes with rich, vivid detail.

- _____ is able to respond to literature in number of ways. I enjoy his/her projects.

## Making Progress

- _____'s comprehension has greatly improved. To help at home, have him/her retell stories as he/she reads them.

- _____ is reading fluently but does not comprehend what he/she reads. When _____ reads at home, ask him/her questions about the story.

- _____ is improving in reading. Thank you for your support.

- _____'s reading is showing improvement. Have him/her read to younger children for additional practice. This should result in further gains.

- _____'s reading is beginning to improve. Continue to expose him/her to a wide variety of materials.

- _____'s reading is slow, but he/she comprehends the text. To increase his/her speed, have him/her orally read the same passage multiple times.

- _____ is learning to attack words independently. He/she is now using more decoding skills.

- _____ can now recognize _____ sight words. Continue using the flashcards for more progress.

- Thank you for talking to _____ about paying attention in class. He/she focuses more on his/her work. As a result, his/her reading has improved.

- _____'s reading is becoming more fluent. Keep reading at home. Your help is appreciated!

- _____ is beginning to read words in phrases; this is helping his/her fluency.

- _____ does well on reading tests, but he/she does not seem to enjoy reading. We need to help him/her develop a love for reading by guiding him/her to books that reflect his/her interests.

- _____ knows all the letters of the alphabet, but I am still concerned about his/her phonemic awareness skills. Please practice rhyming and beginning sounds at home.

# Reading

## Making Progress *(cont.)*

- _____ recognizes most of the uppercase letters, but just a few lowercase letters. Help him/her match uppercase and lowercase letters during flashcard practice to reinforce lowercase recognition.

- _____ is an emergent reader. He/she is showing great effort. Continue reading with him/her at home.

- _____ has improved steadily in reading. He/she is capable of utilizing more reading strategies now.

- _____ can identify sight words in isolation but cannot easily recognize them when reading. More practice is needed.

- _____ now knows and can use the letter sounds. Thank you for your help.

- _____ is gaining independence in reading, however, he/she needs to work towards fluency.

- _____ can decode simple stories but is not reading with expression. He/she needs to practice reading aloud frequently.

- _____ has blossomed this year and is becoming an independent reader. He/she has become more confident in his/her reading abilities.

- _____ is currently reading at grade level, but strengthening his/her comprehension skills will help him/her excel in reading.

- _____ does not understand the importance of phonic skills and depends heavily on sight reading. We need to address this problem so _____ can realize his/her great academic potential.

- I am pleased that _____ has made progress in reading. He/she will soon be on grade level. Thank you for your help.

- _____'s progress has been amazing! His/her reading scores have increased more than anyone's in the class.

- _____'s summarizing skills have improved and as a result, his/her comprehension has improved.

- Through practice, _____ is now able to summarize more effectively.

- _____'s ability to analyze a passage has improved. We will continue to work on this skill in class.

# Reading

## Making Progress (cont.)

- _____ is now able to identify the main ideas in a story in his/her summaries.

- _____ is now able to offer direct responses to his/her reading with reasons, examples, and details.

- _____ now participates in literature circles with more confidence.

- _____'s presentations are more interesting now that he/she uses an outline to organize his/her thoughts.

- _____ is able to analyze the elements of a story and can now draw conclusions.

- _____ is now able to discuss the text, summarize the key points, and make an outline.

## Needs Improvement

- _____ is having difficulty in reading. He/she needs to increase in his/her fluency. Please have him/her read aloud to you each evening.

- _____ is struggling with reading. For him/her to improve, he/she needs to read more at home.

- Although _____ hesitates to read in a group, his/her oral reading is good. Have him/her read aloud at home to build confidence.

- _____ has a great deal of trouble paying attention during reading. I am worried that he/she is missing critical elements. We need to schedule a conference to develop a plan for him/her.

- _____ needs assistance with most reading skills. He/she needs more time devoted to practicing reading skills.

- _____ does not comprehend simple stories. I will be calling for a conference.

- _____ does not willingly participate in reading activities. We need to help him/her develop more skills so reading is easier. We should also help him/her choose interesting books so reading is more enjoyable.

- _____ misinterprets context clues and needs assistance making connections between idea and details. This is affecting his/her comprehension. Have him/her re-tell fairy tales and other familiar stories with as many details as possible to develop this skill.

- _____ is not retaining _____ . He/she needs more repetition and practice at home.

- _____ cannot blend sounds into words. He/she may have an auditory problem. We should have him/her tested.

# Reading

## Needs Improvement *(cont.)*

- _____ is having difficulty with basic phonics skills. I will send home a packet of work that should improve these skills. Please complete it with him/her.

- _____ does not enjoy reading. He/she needs frequent encouragement. Please read with him/her at home to build a love for reading.

- _____ is having difficulty expressing the main idea of a story. I am concerned with his/her level of comprehension. Have him/her identify the main idea of fairy tales or favorite stories to strengthen this skill.

- _____ does not recognize the letters of the alphabet. He/she is working below grade level. Please use the flashcards that I am sending home to practice letter recognition nightly.

- _____ does not recognize rhymes and is struggling to identify initial consonant sounds. Perhaps this is related to his/her speech problems. Continue to provide support at home.

- _____ is weak in basic reading skills. He/she needs to practice alphabet recognition, rhyming, and beginning sounds daily.

- _____ demonstrates letter-sound knowledge. However, he/she cannot yet transfer that knowledge when decoding words. We will continue to practice decoding in small groups.

- With a better attitude toward reading, _____ would enjoy reading more.

- _____ needs to work on vocabulary words more at home. This will help him/her become a better reader.

- _____ does not recognize many sight words. He/she needs to use the flashcards at home.

- _____ is having difficulty with letter sounds. He frequently confuses the sounds of _____ and _____ . Please review sounds at home.

- Please continue working with _____ at home, reading at least 20 minutes a night. Please focus on comprehension strategies. Thank you for your support!

- _____ does not enjoy reading aloud. I won't call on him/her to read in front of a group, but he/she needs to read aloud to you and me to build fluency.

- _____ is struggling with summarizing. Please have him/her practice retelling stories at home.

- _____ has difficulty analyzing his/her reading. We will focus on this during the next grading period.

- _____ makes unsupported responses in the literature circle.

- _____ responds inconsistently and inappropriately in our literature discussions.

# Science

## Proficient

- _____ shows an understanding of all of the scientific concepts we have studied this period.

- _____ is highly engaged in science. He/she uses science materials and equipment correctly to solve problems.

- _____ displays an enthusiasm for science. He/she can predict an outcome and test his/her hypothesis through experimentation. He/she can draw conclusions based on his/her observations.

## Making Progress

- _____ is showing a better understanding of science. He/she participates more in the science activities.

- _____ is applying more skills and strategies and seems to be more aware of safety procedures.

- I am pleased with _____'s progress in science. He/she is making better observations and beginning to record data and show a deeper understanding of the scientific processes.

## Needs Improvement

- _____ does not understand basic science concepts. We need to encourage him/her to take more interest in science.

- _____ needs to pay attention more during our science activities. He/she is easily distracted, and therefore cannot draw conclusions based on observations.

- _____ needs to be encouraged to take risks in scientific endeavors. He/she has difficulty making predictions or drawing conclusions.

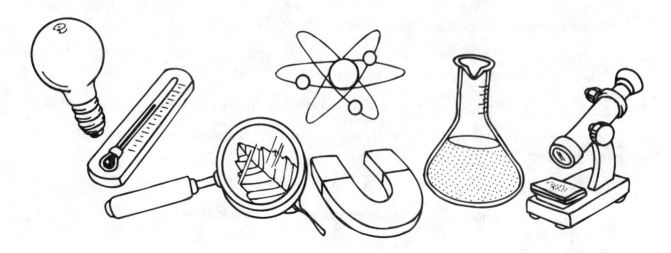

# Social Studies

## Proficient

- _____ communicates the knowledge he/she has gained in social studies. His/her last project was exceptional.

- _____'s reference skills are superior.

- _____ is very interested in current events. This is contributing to him/her becoming a well-rounded citizen.

## Making Progress

- _____ has greatly improved in social studies. However, he/she needs to participate more in classroom discussions.

- _____ is showing a greater interest in social studies. However, he/she did not turn in his/her last project, and this affected his/her grade.

- It is great to see that _____ is showing more effort in social studies. His/her last (map, project, paper, etc.) was delightful.

## Needs Improvement

- _____ has difficulty interpreting maps. Help _____ make simple maps of your home and other familiar places to develop this skill.

- Please encourage _____ to pay better attention during social studies. He/she is off task during our whole-group instruction, and this is affecting his/her ability to complete social studies assignments.

- _____ is not turning in his/her social studies homework. This is affecting his/her grade. Please encourage him/her to complete it and turn it in.

# Spelling

## Proficient

- I am pleased that _____ is serious about spelling. He/she is well prepared for all tests, and this transfers to his/her written work.

- _____ is a great speller! I would like to encourage him/her to try out for the spelling bee. I am sending home a list of words to begin his/her study.

- _____ has achieved excellent scores on our weekly spelling tests.

## Making Progress

- _____'s spelling has greatly improved, but he/she needs to continue working in this subject. Please help him/her practice spelling words nightly.

- Please continue to practice spelling words with _____ . This has made a significant difference in his/her test scores.

- _____ is becoming a great speller. He/she is using an understanding of word families to help him/her spell related words.

## Needs Improvement

- _____ is having a difficult time in spelling. To build success, I would like to give him/her fewer words. Please call me so we can discuss this.

- _____ needs to focus more on his/her spelling words. He/she frequently makes careless errors.

- _____ is struggling in spelling. He/she does not follow any spelling rules, and he/she is not memorizing his/her words. Please review the enclosed spelling rules with _____ and help him/her memorize the weekly spelling list.

# Writing

## Proficient

- _____ utilizes a variety of resources as he/she writes organized and creative stories.

- _____ demonstrates critical thinking in writing. He/she also expresses his/her ideas clearly and concisely.

- _____ excels in writing. He/she drafts ideas fluently, then revises and proofreads to produce a final copy that is accurate, unified, and consistent.

- _____ can self-edit. He/she is ready to publish after editing.

## Making Progress

- I am pleased that _____'s writing has improved. He/she still needs assistance when revising, but he/she is becoming more independent.

- Although _____ needs some help planning and organizing his/her writing, once he/she begins the actual writing he/she is very creative.

- _____ is becoming an accomplished writer. Compare the attached writing samples to notice an overall improvement.

- _____'s editing has improved now that he/she is utilizing more resources.

## Needs Improvement

- _____ does not willingly participate in writing activities. He/she should be encouraged to keep a daily journal or writing log.

- _____ makes many errors in spelling when writing. He/she needs to learn to use resources (spell check, dictionaries, spelling lists, etc.) to correct errors.

- _____ has difficulty organizing information. He/she needs to spend more time planning his/her writing.

- _____ needs a lot of support when editing. He/she cannot find his/her own mistakes.

- To help _____ improve his/her editing skills, I plan to provide opportunities for him to edit with a peer.

# Additional Areas

## Proficient

- _____ enjoys all areas of P.E. He/she displays excellent coordination, agility, and skill.

- _____ responds enthusiastically to all tasks and challenges in P.E. He/she works well with other children and is a well-liked team member.

- _____ is a talented artist. His/her work is colorful and interesting. I hope he/she will continue to study and develop his/her natural ability.

- _____ enjoys art and participates with enthusiasm. His/her work exhibits creativity.

- _____ loves musical activities. If you are able to provide music lessons, he/she would greatly benefit from them.

## Making Progress

- _____ is developing confidence in all areas of P.E. He/she can now _____ .

- _____ is learning to express him/herself through art. As a result, he/she enjoys the class more and is less disruptive.

- _____ is beginning to develop confidence and coordination. If he/she practices _____, he/she will continue to improve.

## Needs Improvement

- _____ is a talented musician. However, his/her lack of dedication is affecting his/her musical development.

- It is obvious when _____ practices at home. Please encourage him/her to schedule a regular practice time if he/she intends to remain involved in music classes.

- _____ has difficulty with his/her coordination and does not seem to enjoy P.E.

- _____ has a natural ability in sports. However, he/she needs to develop sportsmanship.

# Personal Development

Although academic performance comments are essential, a report card is more complete if it also includes remarks about the student's personal development. The explanation for academic performance, in fact, is often directly related to a particular behavior or study skill.

In the following section, the comments address the student's personal development. They can be used in conjunction with academic comments as an explanation or as general, stand-alone comments about the student.

The subjects addressed in this section include attendance and tardiness, attitude toward school, behavior inside and outside, effort in class, self-confidence, social skills, and work habits. Once again, most sections are divided into "Proficient," "Making Progress," and "Needs Improvement" to facilitate the location of an appropriate comment.

# Attendance

## Tardiness

- When _____ is tardy, he/she disturbs the learning of everyone in the classroom. He/she also loses valuable learning time, which is affecting his/her work. Please help _____ arrive in a timely manner.

- Frequent late arrivals affect _____'s academic performance. He/she misses important information each time he/she is late. Your support is needed in this area.

- _____ has been tardy for school _____ times. Because of this, he/she has missed _____ . He/she needs to be at school by _____ A.M. each day.

- _____ is often tardy. Arriving on time for the school day is very important for student success.

- _____ is a joy to teach. He/she arrives at school on time and ready to learn.

## Absences

- _____ learns a lot when present, but frequent absences cause gaps in his/her learning. Please make sure _____ is present each day.

- We need to schedule a time when you can bring _____ to school. Because of his/her frequent absences, I have not been able to completely evaluate his/her progress.

- _____'s frequent absences make it difficult for him/her to stay on grade level. He/she seems tired and often complains about not feeling well. Perhaps _____ should see a doctor.

- Even though _____ completes homework assignments when absent, he/she misses important social interactions and academic activities that make learning complete. Please try to increase _____'s attendance rate.

- _____ has missed _____ days this semester. Because learning is sequential, these absences are affecting his/her academic performance. His/her grades would improve with better attendance.

- _____ is often absent from class. He/she shows promise in _____ but needs to attend regularly to reach his/her potential.

- _____ has been in class and on time every day this grading period. This is reflected in his/her work.

- _____'s attendance is commended. Thank you for your support.

- It is a pleasure to see _____ in class each day. His/her attendance is excellent.

# Attitude

## Proficient

- ____ has made a good adjustment to ____ grade. His/her attitude toward school is excellent.

- ____ is an enthusiastic participant in all of our activities. He/she exhibits a good attitude toward school.

- With ____'s fine attitude and pleasant personality, he/she is a delight to teach.

- ____ assumes responsibility well and has a good attitude. He/she is cooperative and happy.

## Making Progress

- Although ____ has struggled in ____ , he/she has shown a positive attitude about trying to improve in this area.

- ____ is developing a better attitude. He/she now accepts responsibility and is showing interest and enthusiasm for school.

- ____'s attitude is improving since he/she has developed a greater interest in his/her schoolwork. He/she now seems eager to learn.

- I am happy to report that I have seen considerable improvement in ____'s attitude.

## Needs Improvement

- ____ often lacks motivation. If he/she improved his/her classroom attitude and applied more effort, his/her grades would also improve.

- ____ requires a lot supervision. His/her disruptive nature interferes with his/her learning. Please encourage him/her to act more responsibly and develop a better attitude toward school.

- ____ can be very helpful and dependable in the classroom. However, he/she does not always have a good attitude about completing assignments. Please encourage him/her to be more positive about this important aspect of learning.

# Behavior

## Proficient

- _____ is a good citizen. He/she is dependable, responsible, and respectful.

- _____ shares and listens. He/she works well with others.

- _____ is a pleasant, respectful, and well-behaved student.

## Making Progress

- Since our last conference, _____'s behavior has been improving. He/she is showing an interest in his/her schoolwork and seems eager to learn.

- _____ is showing an increased desire to demonstrate appropriate attitude and acceptable behavior in the classroom.

- _____ is learning to anticipate the consequences of his/her actions. This is improving his/her behavior because he/she is taking time to think before acting.

- _____ is learning to react in more socially appropriate ways. Consequently, he/she is making more friends.

- There has been noticeable improvement in _____'s behavior. He/she has made an effort to cooperate with his/her peers and practice self control. Thank you for your support.

- Lately _____ has been working to correct his/her behavior, and I am very proud of him/her. I hope he/she continues to maintain this improvement.

## Needs Improvement

- _____ is very aggressive towards his classmates. Perhaps we should have him/her meet with the school counselor.

- Please encourage _____ to use socially appropriate language at all times.

- Socializing is more important to _____ than classwork. He/she has great potential, but will not realize it until he/she pays better attention in class and focuses more on his/her work.

- _____ can be very disruptive and disorderly. Please encourage him/her to be more responsible in his/her behavior, and call me to schedule a conference.

# Effort

## Proficient

- _____ uses his/her time wisely.  He/she is working to full capacity in all subjects.

- _____ is highly motivated to do his/her personal best.  He/she is a joy to teach!

- _____ is enthusiastic about work and performs well in everything he/she undertakes.

- _____ is a hard worker.  With his/her ability to apply himself/herself, _____ should be successful throughout his/her school career.

## Making Progress

- _____ is becoming more dependable during work periods.  His/her work has improved steadily.

- _____ has made a great effort to improve in his/her schoolwork.

- _____ has shown an encouraging desire to improve.  He/she is making steady progress. Your encouragement is appreciated.

- If _____ will put forth the effort he/she has shown this past grading period, he/she should be on grade level by the end of the year.

- _____ is now demonstrating responsibility by beginning and completing tasks without needing frequent reminders.

## Needs Improvement

- _____'s schoolwork is inconsistent and does not always reflect his/her ability.  If he/she put forth more effort, _____ could work to his/her ability and improve the quality of his/her work.

- _____ does not complete assignments in the allotted time.  He/she needs to apply more effort and learn to pace himself/herself.

- In order for _____ to be successful in school, he/she will need to take responsibility for his/her own work and apply himself/herself to each task.

- _____ needs encouragement and direct supervision to apply effort to his/her work.  I would like to schedule a conference to discuss _____'s progress.

# Outdoor Behavior

## Proficient

- _____ is very athletic and shows good sportsmanship.  Everyone enjoys playing with him/her outside.

- _____ is a leader on the playground.  He/she influences others to make wise choices, organizes games, and invites others to play.

- _____ enjoys physical activity.  He/she uses the playground equipment appropriately and shows good sportsmanship.

## Making Progress

- _____'s behavior is improving outside.  He/she is making better choices and trying to follow the rules.

- _____ is involved in fewer incidences on the playground.  We review outdoor rules every day, and this seems to be making a difference.

- _____ is showing more self-control outside.  He/she is beginning to respect the personal space of other students.

## Needs Improvement

- _____ works well in the classroom.  However, during outside times, he/she finds it difficult to join groups.

- _____ is having trouble on the playground.  The duty personnel report that he/she is disrespectful and uncooperative.  We need to work together to help _____ accept and respect the authority of the adults supervising the playground.

- Occasionally, _____ has problems outside.  This affects his/her classroom demeanor and ability to learn.  Please discuss this matter with him/her.

# Self-Confidence

## Proficient

- _____ is a very happy, well-adjusted child.  He/she speaks with confidence in a group.

- _____ is very confident.  He/she makes friends easily and is well-liked by his/her classmates.

- _____ participates in class and is willing to take risks.  This reflects in his/her academic performance.

## Making Progress

- _____ is gaining more self-confidence.  He/she is beginning to grow in independence.

- _____ is a conscientious student.  He/she is gaining independence, but still needs frequent encouragement.

- _____ has matured nicely.  There is a noticeable improvement in his/her self-confidence, and he/she is now willing to take more risks.

## Needs Improvement

- _____ is anxious to please others. He/she copies others and hesitates to make independent decisions. Please encourage _____ to be more independent, even if he/she makes some mistakes.

- _____ needs a lot of reassurance. He/she gets upset easily and sometimes cries. We need to work on developing his/her confidence so he/she can become more self-reliant.

- _____ hesitates to participate and is unwilling to take risks.  This is affecting his/her academic performance.  We need to persuade him/her to take small risks, then larger ones.  During this period of development, we will need to offer _____ encouragement and support.

# Social Skills

## Proficient

- ＿＿＿ has a pleasant personality. He/she is learning to share, cooperate, and be fair. ＿＿＿ is a great addition to our classroom!

- ＿＿＿ always has time to do something nice for other students. For this reason, he/she is well-liked among his/her peers.

- ＿＿＿ is cheerful and friendly. He/she assumes responsibility, excels in the classroom, and is well-liked by his/her peers.

- ＿＿＿ shows initiative. He/she thinks things through and goes the extra mile on all assignments.

## Making Progress

- ＿＿＿'s social maturity is improving. We need to continue supporting him/her in this area.

- ＿＿＿ is well-liked by his/her peers now that he/she is being friendly and helpful to others.

- I am pleased with the progress that ＿＿＿ is making. He/she has become more cooperative and is learning to work well in groups.

- ＿＿＿ has a great sense of humor that we all enjoy. He/she is now learning when it is more appropriate to be serious.

## Needs Improvement

- ＿＿＿ frequently interrupts others. We will be working to develop patience.

- ＿＿＿ tries to dominate every activity. He/she needs to take turns and be more considerate of others.

- ＿＿＿ has a pleasant personality, but he/she talks constantly. This is affecting his/her academic performance and that of others. Please encourage him/her to be more respectful of his/her learning time and that of others.

- ＿＿＿ is quite reserved around the other students. If possible, provide more opportunities for interaction with peers through a small religious group or other kinds of social groups. Hopefully, this additional contact will help him/her feel more comfortable with other students.

# Work Habits

## Proficient

- _____ is a hard worker and occupies his/her time constructively.

- _____ is working to his/her full potential. He/she is organized and thorough in his/her work.

- _____ works independently on assignments. He/she demonstrates great organizational skills.

- _____ has good organization of thoughts. He/she is a good student who appears to be a deep thinker.

- _____ is a good worker and an attentive listener; he/she is a delight!

## Making Progress

- _____ is learning to use his/her time constructively. Thank you for talking to him/her about this concern.

- Since our last conference, _____ is taking more pride in his/her work. Thank you for your support.

- _____ is beginning to listen more carefully and follow directions. I am expecting continued growth in this area.

- Rather than depending on others, _____ now utilizes a variety of resources to complete his/her assignments.

## Needs Improvement

- _____ needs to concentrate more fully on his/her own work and not be distracted by his/her neighbors. This would result in better work habits and more learning.

- Please encourage _____ to take more care as he/she completes his/her work. It is often disorganized.

- _____ has a lot of potential, but he/she must improve his/her work habits in order to gain the fundamentals needed for _____ grade work.

- Please encourage _____ to focus on his/her work and complete assignments in the allotted time.

# General Messages

Most report card comments focus on academic performance and behavior. However, there are other situations and circumstances that require pertinent observations. A new student's arrival, a homework problem, or a decision about a student's retention may prompt the need for relevant comments.

The General Messages section addresses these and a variety of other situations. Although the headings and comments in this section do not duplicate previous areas, they do overlap them.

Our largest category is devoted to year-end messages. These final comments are extremely important because they summarize the student's progress for the entire year. They often convey a message about what is most important about a student. Year-end comments can reflect the teacher's concern for the student. They can also become part of a lasting record, since the final report card is often saved.

Consequently, final comments should be as positive and hopeful as possible without sending a false message. When improvement is needed, comments should be tactfully phrased to encourage progress. The year-end messages in this section include positive, concise statements, as well as constructive comments that suggest a means to realize potential. To facilitate your use of this category, we have once again used the labels of "Proficient," "Making Progress," and "Needs Improvement."

# Homework

## Proficient

- _____ consistently completes his/her homework. His/her preparation for class is superior.

- I appreciate the way _____ completes homework assignments. His/her work is neat and always on time.

- _____'s homework is always completed carefully and thoughtfully. He/she should be commended for such effort.

## Making Progress

- _____ has taken more care on his/her homework. It is now neat and accurate.

- I can tell that _____ is devoting more effort to his/her homework. It is more accurate and his/her test scores are improving.

- Since _____ has been doing extra homework, he/she has improved in all areas. It is great to see him/her striving to meet his/her potential.

- _____ now turns in his/her homework about 80% of the time. This is a great improvement. Let's work toward 100%!

## Needs Improvement

- _____ needs to put more effort into his/her homework. He/she meets all deadlines, but should be encouraged to improve the quality of his/her work.

- _____ needs to give more attention to his/her homework. It should be completed with more care and turned in on time.

- _____ does not hand in all of his/her homework. He/she is missing _____ assignments. Please talk to him/her about the importance of returning homework.

- _____ has not adequately prepared for our tests. He/she needs to complete his/her homework every day.

- _____ received makeup homework when he/she was absent. The homework was not returned, and this has affected his/her grade. Please have her/him complete and return it.

# New Student

## Proficient

- Although _____ has been in our class for just a short time, he/she has made a great adjustment. The other students enjoy working with him/her, and he/she has made a lot of friends. We are glad he/she joined our class!

- _____ fits in very well in our classroom. He/she has made a good adjustment both socially and academically since he/she joined our class.

- I am so pleased that _____ has moved into our classroom. He/she is a delight!

## Making Progress

- _____ is more adjusted to our class now. He/she seems to understand the work better, and he/she has made some good friends.

- _____ did not seem to enjoy our class during his/her first few weeks here, but I am seeing an improvement now. I think he/she will feel even more comfortable in a few more weeks.

- _____ made friends quickly, but struggled academically during his/her first month in our class. He/she has been steadily improving.

## Needs Improvement

- Since joining our class, _____ has struggled both academically and socially. He/she fights on the playground, and this problem is carrying over into the classroom. Please call for a conference.

- _____ interacts well with the other students. However, he/she is having problems adjusting to the structure of our classroom. Please come in so we can discuss how to help him/her.

- _____ has made a lot of friends since he/she joined our class, but he/she is struggling with the schoolwork. We need to schedule a conference to discuss the curriculum and his/her progress at his/her previous school.

# Above Average Student

- ____ has an excellent attitude. He/she adds to the learning atmosphere in our class.

- ____ uses his/her class time wisely; he/she makes good decisions.

- ____ is working above grade level. His/her achievement is outstanding!

- ____ is an excellent student. He/she has worked hard and excels in all subjects.

- You should be very proud of ____ . He/she is a conscientious student and is always trying to improve his/her skills.

- I can always depend on ____ to set a good example for the rest of the students. It is a pleasure having him/her in my class.

- I have enjoyed having ____ in my class. He/she always makes pertinent and interesting contributions to our class discussions.

- ____ completes his/her work quickly and accurately. He/she is cooperative and attentive. He/she is a delight!

- ____ is gifted; he/she is my top student and can tackle challenges in any academic area.

- ____ is very bright. He/she seeks out new information and learning and consistently challenges himself/herself.

- ____ is a very capable student, but does not like challenges because he/she does not like to fail.

- ____ is a very bright student, but does not work to his/her potential. He/she needs to seek out new learning and challenge himself/herself.

- ____ is an excellent student. However, he/she is too competitive; he/she always has to be first and is unhappy if he/she doesn't win. This has become a problem in our class. Please discuss this at home.

# Average Student

- _____ participates in all of our class activities. The effort he/she applies to his/her work is commendable.

- _____ displays good study skills and works well in a group. He/she shows great interest in our studies and takes pride in his/her work.

- _____ is performing at grade level. His/her daily work is very good.

- _____ is showing satisfactory progress in his/her schoolwork.

- _____ has been working very hard at school. His/her efforts are making a difference. Please encourage him/her to continue.

- _____ has a lot of potential, however, his/her socializing inhibits his/her progress. He/she could improve his/her grades by focusing on his/her work.

- _____ is a dedicated worker and always does his/her best. He/she is having trouble understanding _____ . Please help him/her complete the enclosed work pages.

- _____ has done a good job on his/her (math, reading, writing), however, he/she still struggles with _____ . He/she would benefit from some extra help at home.

- _____ is showing satisfactory progress in all areas. Thank you for encouraging him/her at home.

- I am pleased with the progress that _____ has made. The extra work you are doing at home is making a difference. Please continue _____ .

- I have enjoyed having _____ in my room. He/she is a willing worker with a high interest in everything that we do.

- _____ is a cooperative student and an active participant in our class. His/her basic skills are strong, and he/she is working at grade level.

- _____ is doing satisfactory work; he/she should easily be ready for _____ grade by the end of the year.

# Below Average Student

- In order to improve the quality of his/her work, _____ needs to complete it with more care. He/she also needs to ask for help when he/she struggles with an assignment.

- _____ does not use his/her time effectively, and he/she often daydreams. When he/she learns to pay more attention in class and focus on his/her work, he/she will be more successful.

- _____ needs to develop better organizational skills and study habits. He/she needs to take daily notes and set aside time to study them.

- _____'s last test scores were low. I will let him/her retake the test on _____ . Please help him/her study at home.

- _____'s test scores are low, and he/she does not follow directions. We need to schedule a conference to discuss possible solutions.

- _____ needs to participate in discussions and work to his/her potential.

- _____ has not made enough progress since our last conference. When he/she makes more effort, his/her grades will improve.

- Thank you for coming to conference with me. Our conversation has helped me understand _____ better. Although he/she is struggling, I think our plan will help him/her make progress.

- _____ is always willing to help. Although the work is difficult for him/her, he/she tries everything. Please continue helping him/her at home.

- _____'s work is below grade level. He/she needs to concentrate and develop better study habits.

- I am concerned about _____'s progress. His/her work habits and command of the basic subjects are below grade level. Please help him/her complete all homework assignments.

- _____ tries hard to please, however, he/she is struggling in school. We need to discuss a plan of action. Please call me for a conference.

# Retention

- As you requested, _____ will repeat the _____ grade. I agree that the extra time will be beneficial to him/her.

- _____'s scores are low, and I do not feel he/she will be successful in _____ grade. We need to meet and discuss his/her placement for next year.

- I am considering _____ for retention this year. It is imperative that he/she come to school every day prepared and ready to learn.

- Because of your child's late summer birthday, he/she is not ready for _____ grade. He/she needs another year to mature. As we discussed at our last conference, repeating this grade is in the best interest of your child.

- _____ is a delightful child, but he/she is performing below grade level. Although, he/she is starting to make progress, another year in this grade would greatly benefit him/her.

- I have enjoyed working with _____ this year. He/she has made progress, but is not ready for the rigors of _____ grade. Another year in _____ grade will help strengthen his/her academic foundation.

- _____ is slowly improving in all academic areas. However, he/she is not yet working at grade level. I am concerned whether he/she will be ready for _____ grade by the end of the year. Let's talk about his/her placement in another month.

- Although _____ is ready for _____ grade in most areas, he/she will need to continue the _____ grade reading program until it is completed. He/she will receive additional support next year to ensure success.

- I am happy to report that since _____ was retained last year, he/she has blossomed. He/she has more confidence and is working at grade level.

# Year-End Messages

## Proficient

- It was a pleasure to have _____ in class. He/she is a conscientious worker, as well as a thoughtful, considerate classmate.

- It has been a joy to teach _____ ! He/she is reading easily at a _____ grade level. I expect great things from him/her in the future!

- I have loved being _____'s teacher! He/she is a wonderful student who makes teaching a joy! Thank you for letting me be a part of his/her education. I expect great things from him/her in the future!

- I enjoyed having _____ in my class. He/she demonstrates leadership, accepts responsibility, and takes pride in his/her work.

- It has been a joy to teach _____ ! I will miss his/her enthusiasm and great smile. He/she has made amazing progress this year. I expect great things from him/her!

- _____ has been a joy to teach! He/she has made amazing progress and is ready for _____ grade. Thank you for the privilege of being his/her teacher.

- _____ is a model student; he/she is bright, dedicated, and self-disciplined. Thank you for the opportunity to teach such a delightful child!

- It has been a joy to teach _____; he/she is so full of wonder and personality! He/she has made great progress this year in all areas.

- I have enjoyed teaching _____ . He/she is a smart girl/boy who is ready for _____ grade. He/she is also a class leader with many friends. Enjoy your summer with him/her!

- _____ has been a joy to teach! He/she has worked very hard and made great progress this year. He/she has a natural curiosity and a great desire to learn! Best of luck in _____ grade.

- I have truly enjoyed teaching _____ ; he/she is a reflection of great parents. _____ made great academic progress and is ready to advance. I will miss the _____ family!

- It was a pleasure to teach _____ this year. He/she is cooperative, courteous, and considerate of others.

- I have loved teaching _____ . He/she has been an eager learner and an active participant in all that we have done. He/she should not have any trouble in _____ grade.

# Year-End Messages

## Proficient *(cont.)*

- I have enjoyed having _____ in class. He/she works diligently and gets along with the other students. His/her _____ skills are solid, and he/she is reading at a _____ grade level.

- _____ accomplished a lot this year; his/her skills are strong and he/she is reading fluently. He/she is an active participant in the learning process. _____ is a joy to teach!

- I am glad _____ was in my class. His/her academic skills are strong, and he/she has the potential for developing strong leadership skills. He/she is a great student!

- _____ is ready for any challenge. He/she is reading _____ grade material and working above grade level in many areas. _____ is friendly, outgoing, and enthusiastic. I have enjoyed being his/her teacher!

- _____ is an extraordinary girl/boy. He/she participates in all activities and works well with the other students. _____ made great progress and should enjoy _____ grade. I have enjoyed being his/her teacher!

- _____ has strong academic skills. He/she is working above grade level in all areas.

- _____ is popular, helpful, and ready for anything! I am glad he/she was in my class.

- _____ has been a lot of fun this year. He/she has a love of learning that is pushing him/her to the top of the class. He/she has been an asset to our classroom.

- It has been a pleasure to have _____ in class this year. With his/her continued effort and excellence, he/she will receive much satisfaction.

- _____ has made this a pleasant year. His/her progress has been impressive! Thank you for your support and interest. Have a wonderful summer!

- I enjoyed having _____ in class. He/she has a great sense of humor and gets along well with his/her peers. I have high expectations for him/her in the future.

- _____ has been a wonderful addition to our class! He/she has been a friendly, cooperative, and enthusiastic learner.

- _____ has made great progress this year. His/her effort in our class was impressive! I hope this attitude and effort will carry over to the next school year.

- _____ is a conscientious student who should have much success in school. His/her friendly, sincere way has made him/her very popular. It has been a pleasure to have him/her in my class.

# Year-End Messages

## Proficient *(cont.)*

- _____ has been a fine citizen and a constant contributor. I am sure he/she will be very successful next year.

- _____ takes pride in his/her work; it is always neat and thorough. His/her work habits are impressive and his skills are strong. I have enjoyed being his/her teacher.

- _____ has earned a fine report card this semester. He/she is cooperative, happy, and a good citizen. _____ is a dedicated student, and I expect him/her to excel in _____ grade.

- _____ made steady progress in all areas this year. He/she is definitely ready for _____ grade. _____ has a high interest in learning. I have enjoyed being his/her teacher.

- _____ is a delightful boy/girl. He/she has strong skills in all areas. _____ is enthusiastic about learning. I have loved being his/her teacher.

## Making Progress

- It has been a treat to have _____ in my classroom. There has been a noticeable improvement in his/her work. With continued effort, he/she will have great success in school.

- _____ is a fine citizen and a hard worker. I have enjoyed watching him/her blossom this year. With continued effort, he/she should do well in school.

- _____ has done well in school. Practice his/her skills this summer to keep him/her prepared for _____ grade. It has been a joy to teach _____ ; he/she has a great personality!

- I have loved teaching _____ . He/she has worked diligently, made great progress, and is ready for _____ grade.

- _____ has matured nicely this year. He/she takes an interest in his/her work and always does his/her personal best.

- _____ has made wonderful academic progress and is well on his/her way to reading. It has been a joy to be his/her teacher!

- _____ is a great student! I have truly enjoyed being his/her teacher. He/she has worked very hard and made great progress. With continued support, he/she should do well in _____ grade.

- _____ is now at grade level! He/she needs to practice this summer to keep his/her skills sharp. I have loved being his/her teacher.

# Year-End Messages

## Making Progress *(cont.)*

- _____ is always eager to help his/her classmates; he/she has the potential to be a leader. _____ has improved steadily throughout the year. It has been a privilege to teach him/her.

- _____ made continual progress this year. His/her interest in our classroom activities steadily increased; at the same time his/her skills improved. Thank you for helping at home.

- _____ has had to work at every stage, but he/she has been willing to put forth the effort. He/she is on grade level, but continue practicing _____ this summer to maintain skills. _____ is a great student!

## Needs Improvement

- I enjoyed teaching _____ . He/she made a lot of improvement this year, but is still working below grade level. The class requirements will need to be modified again next year.

- _____ is a delightful girl/boy. He/she made a lot of improvement, but needs to practice reading every day this summer. Please continue reviewing math skills also. I have enjoyed being his/her teacher; good luck in _____ grade.

- In order for _____ to be ready for _____ grade this fall, please continue to practice and review skills at home. I have enclosed a packet of summer homework that highlights the skills that still need to be mastered.

- I am afraid that _____ is going to struggle in _____ grade. Although his/her academic skills are at grade level, he/she has had a difficult time behaving. This is going to affect his/her learning as well as distract the rest of the class. Please try some of the strategies we have used throughout the year to reinforce better behavior.

# Words and Phrases

After choosing comments from this book, you may want to extend some of them. The Words and Phrases section serves as an excellent resource for augmenting report card comments.

As you complete a comment for a student, facts and examples can be added to substantiate it. By selecting words or phrases that are most appropriate, you can develop a comment that accurately and specifically describes a student or situation.

The lists in the Words and Phrases section can assist you in personalizing your comments. You can use the same reading comment for a number of students, then individualize each with a different set of words or phrases.

The Words and Phrases section can also inspire and guide you as you write your own comments. The suggested words can help you effectively create comments that are interesting and meaningful.

To facilitate the use of this section, the lists are divided into the following categories:

- Academics
- Attitude
- Behavior
- Communication
- Connecting with Families
- Creativity
- General
- Helpful Adjectives
- Helpful Verbs
- Two-Word Phrases
- Work Habits

# Academics

## Proficient

- I am excited to see progress in _____

- demonstrates depth and insight in writing

- I am trying to help _____ by _____

- _____ is a high achiever

- demonstrates a high level of competence

- utilizes successful strategies

- greatly skilled in _____

- methodical in solving problems

- excels in analytical thinking

- concentrates on analyzing facts

- is working well in all subjects

- highly skilled in _____

- demonstrates a high level of expertise

- possesses high expertise in _____

- excels in assisting others with _____

- displays a high sense of inquiry

- displays a strong power of observation

- completes projects with impressive results

- contributes thoughtful comments to _____ discussions

- capable of reading demanding texts

- chooses to read during free time

- willingly takes suggestions from peers and teacher

- self-edits during the writing process

- produces highly accurate work

# Academics

## Making Progress

- working harder now to meet academic goals

- makes better use of resources

- more fully prepared

- is developing correct capitalization and punctuation

- now requires a minimum of guidance when completing assignments

- continuously strives to strengthen _____

- consistently strives to improve performance

- is now organizing work well

- is more orderly and systematic

## Needs Improvement

- with greater effort, he/she can improve his/her _____

- as he/she continues to mature academically, _____ will experience greater success

- thinking outside of the box is a challenge

- needs to develop stronger skills in _____

- needs to be encouraged to take risks in writing

- needs strengthening in _____ skills

- struggling to understand the concepts of _____

- could exceed grade level goals with greater effort

- needs to be encouraged to read

- needs help using reference books

- needs to be encouraged to successfully complete all assignments

- is not working to his/her potential

# Connecting with Families

- we need to schedule a conference

- please call for an appointment

- feel free to call for an appointment

- thank you for your help

- I appreciate your willingness to help

- I appreciate your support

- thank you for practicing daily on _____ at home

- please encourage your child to _____

- thank you for volunteering to help in our class

- your continual support has helped _____ improve in _____

- has benefited from consistent parent-teacher communication

- looking forward to seeing you at our learning night

- please call if you have questions or concerns

- thank you for being a partner in _____'s education

- your help is greatly appreciated

- glad you were able to attend the parent night

- your help has benefited everyone in our classroom

# Work Habits

## Proficient

- demonstrates a high level of independence
- excellent work is a reflection of his/her effort
- seeks out highly challenging tasks
- outstanding organizational skills

- displays good study skills
- displays a strong sense of priorities
- uses time wisely

- recognizes the importance of accuracy
- strives for perfection
- meticulous with details

- makes effective use of _____
- effectively uses technology
- shows maximum effort
- excels in self-pacing

- motivated to achieve high standards
- displays an enthusiastic spirit
- displays an intense desire
- goes beyond what is expected

- is totally absorbed in school
- is success-oriented
- is not content with mediocrity
- works well with others

- plans appropriate strategies to arrive at solutions
- takes initiative in solving problems
- anticipates opportunities
- develops positive strategies

# Work Habits

## Making Progress

- should be encouraged to _____
- is learning to listen carefully
- ____'s determination and effort have raised his/her grades
- is working toward becoming conscientious in completing his/her work
- is gaining independence in _____
- displays a willingness to make improvements
- better at sustaining concentration now
- now gives maximum effort
- is more task-oriented
- completing tasks in an efficient manner now
- now capable of assuming greater responsibility

## Needs Improvement

- rarely participates in discussions
- needs continual guidance and supervision
- needs highly-structured directions
- ____'s note-taking needs improvement
- needs to take pride in his/her work
- does not complete assignments on time
- needs to concentrate on his/her own work
- needs to learn to contribute in a more appropriate manner
- constantly seeks teacher assistance
- needs more consistent practice
- excessive tardies and absences
- encourage him/her to strive for quality work
- needs to complete assignments with more care
- inclined to be dependent on others for directions

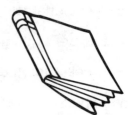

# General

## Proficient

- impresses me with his/her focus
- is a pleasure to have in class
- a creative problem solver
- makes fine contributions to our class
- is intuitive

- continues to amaze me with his/her insights
- is very compassionate
- conscientious, hardworking student

- has a wonderful sense of humor
- is friendly and cooperative
- is well-spoken

- is well-liked by his/her classmates
- demonstrates incredible leadership skills
- has blossomed this year
- bubbles over with enthusiasm
- an energetic participant in all activities

- is dependable in carrying out responsibilities
- displays diligence in performing tasks
- can be relied upon

- displays a strong commitment to successfully completing projects
- displays a strong capacity for growth

- has a great deal of energy and enthusiasm
- always makes time to assist others
- is a joy to have in class
- always willing to give extra effort
- benefits from constructive criticism

# General

## Proficient *(cont.)*

- sets ambitious goals
- is a self-starter
- takes initiative in solving problems
- seizes all opportunities
- plans and organizes with little or no assistance

- demonstrates innovative insight
- makes a favorable impression

- is accepted by others
- establishes effective working relationships
- promotes harmony among classmates

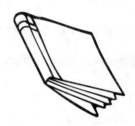

- exercises considerable influence within the group
- interacts effectively with peers
- clearly understands objectives and procedures
- is exceptionally well-informed
- projects self-confidence and enthusiasm

- displays an exceptional ability to learn
- is totally committed to achieving excellence
- works with enthusiasm

- is able to overcome extreme difficulties
- is task-oriented
- ambitious and high-spirited

- displays a pleasant, cheerful disposition
- possesses all traits associated with excellence
- displays a pleasing personality
- has an outgoing personality
- brings a fresh perspective into our classroom

# General

## Making Progress

- is more reliable now when given an assignment

- could profit by _____

- beginning to blossom in all areas

- developing a sense of responsibility towards his/her learning

- shows improvement in making contributions to class projects

- displays a willingness to make improvements

- uses suggestions to improve performance

- displays an eagerness to improve

- shows steady progress

- continues to grow and improve

- demonstrates an ability to relate to his/her classmates

- demonstrates a better understanding of procedures

- is showing more leadership skills

- is more receptive to new ideas

- beginning to grasp new routines

- showing more effort to maintain skills

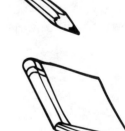

- displays a renewed sense of purpose

- is now demonstrating independent thinking

- is displaying a stronger commitment to _____

- projects more energy and enthusiasm

# General

## Needs Improvement

- should be encouraged to _____

- needs to accept responsibility for his/her actions

- has difficulty with _____

- appears inattentive

- takes action too hastily

- needs constant reassurance

- needs to be more open-minded

- needs more hands-on experiences

- relies too heavily on others

- emulates peers instead of making independent decisions

- needs encouragement to achieve potential

- shows little enthusiasm for learning

- needs to learn from mistakes

- needs to take more pride in work

- needs to be encouraged to use common sense

- would improve performance with more study

- needs encouragement to develop leadership skills

# Behavior

## Proficient

- demonstrates good judgment

- promotes cooperative behavior and team effort

- is conscientious

- is an involved learner

- cooperates with his/her peers

- displays a high degree of integrity

- exhibits a high degree of emotional maturity

- presents different opinions without creating conflicts

- handles confrontations with tact

- is very cordial/polite

- is sincere

- excels in developing "what if" scenarios

- always has a smile on his/her face

- greatly focused on work

- is a class leader

- is a determined learner

- is a dependable student

- demonstrates empathy toward his/her classmates

# Behavior

## Making Progress

- is beginning to be responsible for staying on task

- participates more fully when monitored by the teacher

- has become more cooperative

- is now maintaining attention to the task at hand

- is making wiser choices

- much improved behavior

- is becoming more self-reliant

- keeps anger under better control

- is becoming more flexible

- is beginning to participate more

- is showing more consideration for others' feelings

- is becoming more patient

- is more focused on work

- is developing leadership skills

- requires less teacher supervision during independent work time

# Behavior

## Needs Improvement

- manages his/her peers too much

- his/her socialization inhibits academic progress

- finds it difficult to make a smooth transition between activities

- needs to display a more cooperative nature

- needs to develop a calmer temperament

- follows school rules only when closely monitored

- has difficulty following directions

- needs to develop self-control

- showing minimal improvement since our last grading period

- requires a lot of supervision

- avoids emotional involvement

- needs to cope constructively with emotions

- needs to think before taking action

- needs to know appropriate times to speak

- needs to take responsibility for his/her actions

- requires guidance and supervision to minimize disruptive behavior

- has trouble functioning in group settings

- needs to use humor constructively

- capable of assuming a greater leadership role

- successful within a consistent structure

- challenged during work time by his/her social nature

# Communication

## Proficient

- communicates clearly and concisely
- excels in interpersonal communications
- asks pertinent questions
- listens carefully
- effectively communicates ideas
- effectively explains and interprets _____
- is a polished and confident speaker
- makes effective demonstrations
- effectively uses an extensive vocabulary
- is highly articulate
- makes persuasive presentations

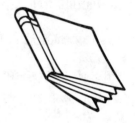

## Making Progress

- is beginning to listen consistently
- is now communicating with ease
- his/her language is more relevant and meaningful
- expresses ideas more clearly
- his/her questions are more pertinent
- is displaying more self-confidence when speaking
- uses an increasing vocabulary

## Needs Improvement

- responds slowly to oral and written directions
- needs to develop a stronger vocabulary
- needs to communicate with confidence
- needs to use concise and clear language
- needs to state position clearly
- needs to develop better listening skills
- should seek out more opportunities for public speaking

# Attitude

## Proficient

- has a positive attitude towards school
- shows genuine interest in _____
- is eager to participate in _____
- explores new opportunities
- is eager to try new approaches
- effectively applies new concepts and techniques
- has incredible energy and enthusiasm
- displays multifaceted vision
- focuses on the future

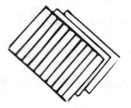

## Making Progress

- is showing an improved attitude
- improved report card reflects his/her attitude toward school
- displaying more self-confidence
- is showing more interest in _____
- now sees the connection between learning and his/her future
- is exhibiting more initiative
- greatly improved level of participation

## Needs Improvement

- responds slowly
- needs to improve attitude
- lacks self-confidence
- would benefit from trying new approaches
- needs to direct incredible energy toward learning
- needs to seize opportunities to participate
- needs to show more interest in _____

# Creativity

## Proficient

- displays creative imagination
- excels in creative thinking and problem solving
- successfully develops creative strategies
- is very creative
- demonstrates a high degree of originality
- possesses many talents and capabilities
- possesses a unique combination of skill and talent
- extremely versatile

## Making Progress

- has started thinking "outside the box"
- is beginning to seek creative alternatives
- is beginning to use imagination to solve problems
- is becoming aware of hidden talents
- is showing more originality and creativity
- now initiates fresh ideas
- is willing to take more risks
- is beginning to nurture his/her curiosity

## Needs Improvement

- encourage _____ to take risks and explore new ideas
- encourage him/her to explore new paths and procedures
- needs to direct considerable energy to creatively solving problems
- needs guidance to effectively use creative talents
- would benefit from lessons to develop creative ability
- active imagination needs guidance
- has the ability to be original
- high degree of creativity not being realized

# Two-Word Phrases

- challenging problems

- basic strengths

- achieving excellence

- accepting responsibility

- accomplishing results

- achievement-oriented

- analytical reasoning

- clear expectations

- competent performer

- confident speaker

- creative solutions

- creative strengths

- developing solutions

- driving force

- dynamic impressions

- efficient manner

- enthusiastic spirit

- exciting challenge

- extremely resourceful

- favorable impression

- fresh enthusiasm

- genuine interest

- goal seeker

- high achiever

- high potential

- highly articulate

- highly committed

- highly competent

- highly energized

- imaginative thinking

# Two-Word Phrases

- important contributor
- impressive results
- independent decisions
- inner drive
- innovative thinking
- intense desire
- leadership qualities
- learning opportunities
- maximum effort
- measurable results
- mental toughness
- new approaches
- open-minded
- optimal results

- peak efficiency
- personal integrity
- pleasing personality
- positive attitude
- practical thinking
- proven performer
- self-starter
- solid achiever
- strong effort
- success-oriented
- team motivator
- unique solutions
- visionary thinker
- works effectively

# Helpful Adjectives

- abundant
- active
- adept
- alert
- ambitious
- articulate
- calm
- capable
- challenging
- compelling
- competent
- confident
- courteous
- curious
- dedicated
- dependable
- diligent
- distinctive
- dynamic
- efficient

- energetic
- enthusiastic
- exceptional
- extraordinary
- fair
- fine
- forceful
- genuine
- great
- helpful
- honest
- imaginative
- independent
- industrious
- innovative
- knowledgeable
- logical
- loyal
- magnificent
- mature

# Helpful Adjectives

- motivated
- observant
- optimistic
- organized
- original
- outstanding
- perceptive
- persuasive
- pleasant
- positive
- productive
- punctual
- realistic
- remarkable
- resourceful
- respectful
- self-confident
- significant
- splendid

- stimulating
- strong
- successful
- superb
- superior
- supportive
- tactful
- thorough
- trustworthy
- ultimate
- understanding
- unique
- unusual
- versatile
- vibrant
- vigorous
- well-liked
- winning
- zestful

# Helpful Verbs

- accelerates
- accepts
- accomplishes
- achieves
- acquires
- adapts
- addresses
- adjusts
- analyzes
- anticipates
- applies
- articulates
- ascertains
- aspires
- asserts
- assumes
- attempts
- augments
- broadens
- builds

- calculates
- capitalizes
- challenges
- clarifies
- collaborates
- communicates
- completes
- comprehends
- computes
- concentrates
- concludes
- considers
- contemplates
- controls
- cooperates
- creates
- defines
- delivers
- demonstrates
- deserves

- designs
- develops
- discovers
- displays
- earns
- emphasizes
- empowers
- encourages
- energizes
- excels
- extends
- facilitates
- follows-up
- foresees
- formulates
- fulfills
- gains
- grasps
- generates
- identifies

# Helpful Verbs

- impacts
- implements
- impresses
- improves
- increases
- informs
- inspires
- instructs
- integrates
- interacts
- interprets
- introduces
- investigates
- knows
- launches
- leads
- learns
- maintains
- maximizes
- modifies

- motivates
- necessitates
- notifies
- observes
- obtains
- operates
- organizes
- overcomes
- participates
- possesses
- practices
- prioritizes
- projects
- provides
- realizes
- recalls
- recognizes
- recommends
- records
- reflects

- reinforces
- represents
- requires
- resolves
- reviews
- seeks
- simplifies
- solves
- strengthens
- strives
- suggests
- supports
- surpasses
- sustains
- thinks
- understands
- unifies
- utilizes
- verifies
- weighs